Can Zac See?

By Sally Cowan

Zac and Max run in the fog.

Max! Can you see the red fox?

Mum and Zac mix and mix.

But Zac did not get a bag.

He got a box!

Zac got in Mum's van.

He went to see Doc Yin.

Zac sits and looks.

He can see dots
and zig zags.

Doc Yin got a big box.

Zac can not see a lot.
But we can fix it!

CHECKING FOR MEANING

1. What did Zac think was a red fox? *(Literal)*

2. What was in the box that Zac thought was nuts? *(Literal)*

3. Why was Zac able to see better at the end of the story? *(Inferential)*

EXTENDING VOCABULARY

zig zags	What are *zig zags*? Where might you see them? Why do you think this pattern is called a *zig zag*?
fox	What words do you know that describe a *fox*? How would it feel to pat a fox? Does a fox move quickly or slowly?
fix	Which letter in the word *fix* is not in the word *fox*? If you took the *f* away from the start of *fix* and put another letter at the start, what word could you make?

MOVING BEYOND THE TEXT

1. What are some reasons people wear glasses?

2. If you can't see well, why is it important to have glasses to see better?

3. Do you think Zac will enjoy wearing his glasses? Why?

4. Which workers do you know that wear glasses to protect their eyes?

SPEED SOUNDS

Xx	Yy	Zz				
Kk	Ll	Vv	Qq	Ww		
Dd	Jj	Oo	Gg	Uu		
Cc	Bb	Rr	Ee	Ff	Hh	Nn
Mm	Ss	Aa	Pp	Ii	Tt	

PRACTICE WORDS

Max

Zac

fox

mix

Yap

Yes

box

Yin

zig

zags

fix

yap